A NOTE TO PAREN

Reading Aloud with Your Child

Research shows that reading books aloud is the single most valuable support parents can provide in helping children learn to read.

- Be a ham! The more enthusiasm you display, the more your child will enjoy the book.
- Run your finger underneath the words as you read to signal that the print carries the story.
- Leave time for examining the illustrations more closely; encourage your child to find things in the pictures.
- Invite your youngster to join in whenever there's a repeated phrase in the text.
- Link up events in the book with similar events in your child's life.
- If your child asks a question, stop and answer it. The book can be a means to learning more about your child's thoughts.

Listening to Your Child Read Aloud

The support of your attention and praise is absolutely crucial to your child's continuing efforts to learn to read.

- If your child is learning to read and asks for a word, give it immediately so that the meaning of the story is not interrupted. DO NOT ask your child to sound out the word.
- On the other hand, if your child initiates the act of sounding out, don't intervene.
- If your child is reading along and makes what is called a miscue, listen for the sense of the miscue. If the word "road" is substituted for the word "street," for instance, no meaning is lost. Don't stop the reading for a correction.
- If the miscue makes no sense (for example, "horse" for "house"), ask your child to reread the sentence because you're not sure you understand what's just been read.
- Above all else, enjoy your child's growing command of print and make sure you give lots of praise. *You are your child's first teacher — and the most important one. Praise from you is critical for further risk-taking and learning.*

— Priscilla Lynch
Ph.D., New York University
Educational Consultant

For Daniel
—F.R.

For Sam
—J.D.Z.

Library of Congress Cataloging-in-Publication Data

Robinson, Fay.
    Great snakes! / by Fay Robinson ; illustrated by Jean Day Zallinger
            p.   cm. — (Hello reader! Level 2)
                    ISBN 0-590-26243-2
        1. Snakes — Juvenile literature. [1. Snakes.]   I. Zallinger, Jean, ill.
II. Title.   III. Series.
QL666.06R485   1996   95-10531
597.96 — dc20   CIP
                                                                       AC

12 11 10 9 8 7 6   8 9/9 0 1/0

                    Printed in the U.S.A.   23

            First Scholastic printing, May 1996

Great Snakes!

by Fay Robinson
Illustrated by Jean Day Zallinger

Hello Science Reader!— Level 2

SCHOLASTIC INC.
New York Toronto London Auckland Sydney

Two snakes.

Four snakes.

Six snakes.

Eight.

Every single snake is great!

Snakes with diamonds,

stripes,

and dots.

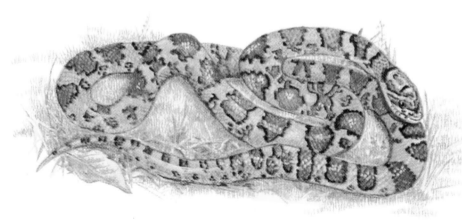

Snakes with many
kinds of spots.

Snakes in deserts.

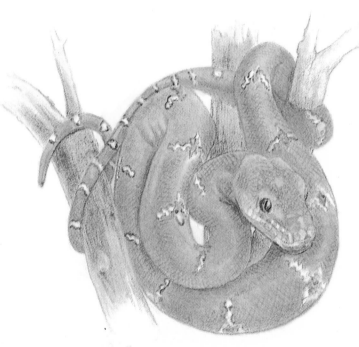

Snakes in trees.

Snakes in mountains.

Snakes in seas.

With no legs,
snakes climb

and slide.

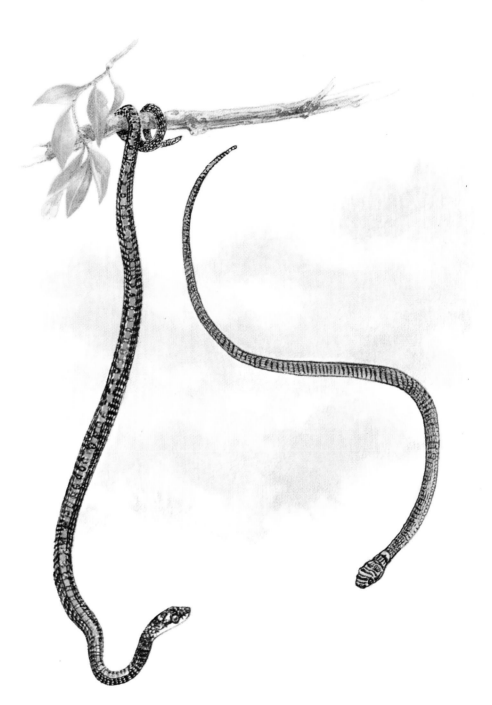

There are snakes
that hang, then glide.

Scaly skin is rough

or soft.

When it's old,
it peels right off.

Snakes with fangs—

a scary sight.

Snakes with fangs
have poison bites!

Snakes that
coil small.

Snakes that
stretch tall.

Round and thick snakes.

Thin-like-sticks snakes.

Snakes with flat snouts.

Forked tongues flick out.

Snake eggs.

One snake.

Two snakes.

Three.

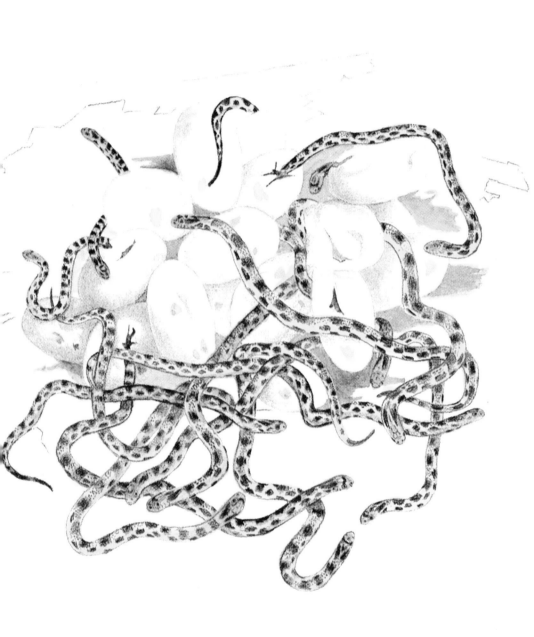

Now how many
do you see?

Snakes with rattles.

Snakes in battles.

Snakes that play dead.

Snakes with two heads.

Two snakes.

Four snakes.

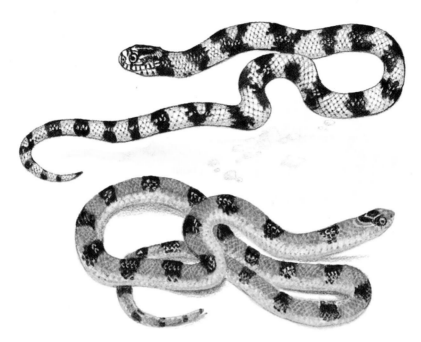

Six snakes.

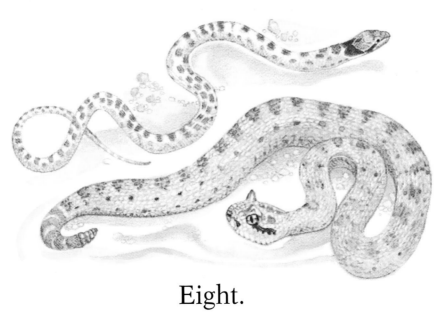

Eight.
Every single
snake is great!